SOCCER

UNDERDOG STORIES

BY SAM MOUSSAVI

UNDERDOG
SPORTS STORIES

SportsZone

An Imprint of Abdo Publishing | abdobooks.com

abdobooks.com

Published by Abdo Publishing, a division of ABDO, PO Box 398166, Minneapolis, Minnesota 55439.

Printed in the United States of America, North Mankato, Minnesota
092018
012019

THIS BOOK CONTAINS
RECYCLED MATERIALS

Cover Photo: Rui Vieira/AP Images
Interior Photos: Staff/AFP/Getty Images, 5; EMPICS Sport/PA Images/Getty Images, 6; AP Images, 8; PA Images/Getty Images, 11, 12; PA Wire/AP Images, 14; Tommy Cheng/AFP/Getty Images, 17, 18; Gilbert Iundt/Corbis Historical/Getty Images, 20; Jay LaPrete/AP Images, 23; Ben Radford/Getty Images Sport/Getty Images, 24; Marcio Jose Sanchez/AP Images, 27; Rui Vieira/AP Images, 29; Robin Parker/Cal Sport Media/AP Images, 30; David Klein/Cal Sport Media/AP Images, 33; Luis Acosta/AFP/Getty Images, 35; Manu Fernandez/AP Images, 36; Bernat Armangue/AP Images, 38; Ed Nessen/AP Images, 41; Lenny Ignelzi/AP Images, 43; Sean Brown/Cal Sports Media/AP Images, 45

Editor: Patrick Donnelly
Series Designer: Melissa Martin

Library of Congress Control Number: 2018949201

Publisher's Cataloging-in-Publication Data

Names: Moussavi, Sam, author.
Title: Soccer underdog stories / by Sam Moussavi.
Description: Minneapolis, Minnesota : Abdo Publishing, 2019 | Series: Underdog sports stories | Includes online resources and index.
Identifiers: ISBN 9781532117640 (lib. bdg.) | ISBN 9781532170508 (ebook)
Subjects: LCSH: Soccer--Juvenile literature. | Upsets in sports--Juvenile literature. | Winning and losing--Juvenile literature.
Classification: DDC 796.334--dc23

TABLE OF CONTENTS

CHAPTER 1

CONTINENTAL UPRISING

An underdog can be a team that is given little to no chance to win. Or it can be an athlete who has overcome major challenges. The history of sports provides many examples of underdogs. Soccer has given the world some of its biggest thrills along with some of the most memorable stories.

One of them took place on June 29, 1950. Soccer fans call it "the Miracle on Grass." The US men's team went into their World Cup match against England that day as

England's Thomas Finney, *center*, fights for the ball with American defenders Charlie Colombo (4) and Ed McIlvenny.

heavy underdogs. England was a heavy favorite to win the tournament, which took place in Brazil that year. Though the US team was making its third World Cup appearance and England its first, the English had the upper hand. England had some of the best players in the world, including forwards Tom Finney and Stan Mortensen. The US squad was made up of part-time players who also held other jobs such as teacher, mailman, and funeral director.

The US team poses for a photo before its match against heavily favored England.

The match was the second of the tournament for both teams. England won its first group stage game against Chile 2–0. The US lost its first match to Spain 3–1. England wasted no time against the Americans, taking control with several early scoring chances. "For the first 20 minutes, England were all over us," US captain Walter Bahr said. US goalkeeper Frank Borghi was busy early. England had six shots on goal by the 12th minute. The US team did not get its first shot on goal until 25 minutes into the match. It was clear the Americans had their work cut out for them.

MATTHEWS MISSING

England's Stanley Matthews was one of the world's top players in 1950. He missed the first game of the World Cup but was available to play against the United States. However, the team's selection committee didn't want to change the lineup, so Matthews sat out. And with no substitutions allowed at the time, he was unable to help his team avoid the upset.

Excited fans carry Joe Gaetjens off the field after his goal helped the United States upset England 1–0 at the 1950 World Cup.

Then the improbable happened during the 37th minute. American forward Joe Gaetjens snuck the ball past English keeper Bert Williams to take a 1–0 lead. England had a few more scoring chances in the first half but could not come up with the equalizer.

The US team played with confidence on both sides of the ball as the second half began. The Americans nearly doubled their lead with an early scoring chance. Then Borghi turned away a free kick from Mortensen during the 59th minute. England had only one other good chance late in the match, but Borghi tipped the shot away at the last second. After that the final whistle sounded, and the 1–0 victory was sealed.

It was a stunning upset to sports fans around the globe. But because soccer hadn't yet become popular in the United States, the impact of the win would not be felt at home until much later. "At the time, I didn't realize how big a victory it really was," Bahr said during an interview to celebrate the fiftieth anniversary of the win over England.

CHAPTER 2

NEWCOMER MAKES WAVES

The 1966 World Cup took place in England. Italy's qualification for the tournament was no surprise. The Italians were making their sixth World Cup appearance since 1934. North Korea, the only Asian country to qualify, was playing in its first World Cup.

Not much was expected from the North Koreans, whose opponents in group play were Chile, Italy, and the Soviet Union. Italy and the Soviet Union were favored to advance to the knockout stage. Few even acknowledged

A British sailor walks off the field celebrating with Pak Seung-Zin after North Korea drew with Chile in the 1966 World Cup.

North Korea's presence. A 3–0 loss to the Soviet Union in its first match was right in line with expectations. North Korea was overpowered, and the match was essentially over by halftime.

In its second match, however, North Korea fared better. Trailing Chile 1–0, North Korea was able to equalize in the 88th minute with a goal by Pak Seung-Zin. The spirited effort inspired some English fans to root for North Korea.

Pak Doo-Ik, *left*, scores the winning goal against Italy at Ayresome Park in Middlesbrough, England.

There was something inspiring about the squad from North Korea. The team played hard and played until the end. The 1–1 draw against Chile showed the world that North Korea could compete. But the team faced long odds in its final group match against Italy.

The Italian team, also known as "the *Azzurri*" for their blue jerseys, beat Chile but lost a tough second match to the Soviet Union. That meant the match against North Korea was important to both sides. A trip to the knockout stage was on the line.

Italy only needed a draw to move on, but the *Azzurri* played to win. They narrowly missed two early scoring chances, but the North Koreans did not back down. They attacked the Italian defensive line, creating a few scoring chances for themselves.

Italy was dealt a massive blow about 30 minutes into the game. Midfielder Giacomo Bulgarelli was injured while making a sliding tackle and had to leave the game. At the time, substitutes were not allowed in international play. That meant Italy had to finish the game with 10 players.

The real shock happened about 12 minutes later. Pak Doo-Ik scored a goal on a perfectly headed pass from a teammate. North Korea took an improbable 1–0 lead on Italy. A massive upset was in the making. Italy had chances to tie the game in the second half, but no one

Portuguese star Eusébio scores one of his four goals against North Korea in the World Cup quarterfinals.

on the Azzurri side could deliver. With the 1–0 victory North Korea moved onto the knockout stage while Italy went home.

England went on to win the World Cup in front of its home fans, defeating West Germany 4–2 in a memorable final at Wembley Stadium in London. But North Korea's victory over Italy remains an important part of World Cup history. The tiny underdogs from Asia defeated a world power. It's still the biggest win in North Korea's history.

PORTUGAL RALLIES

North Korea was not finished making waves. Facing another giant in Portugal in the knockout stage, the dream continued as North Korea built a 3–0 lead in just 25 minutes. But Portugal stormed back behind the genius of striker Eusébio. He scored four goals to help the favorites take the lead. Portugal defeated North Korea 5–3, ending the underdog's magical run.

CHAPTER 3

MAKING HISTORY

The first World Cup was played in Uruguay in 1930. Of course, that was only for men. It would be another half-century before women's soccer could establish a foothold in the sports world. International teams began forming in the 1980s, and by the end of the decade the idea of a World Cup for women was gaining popularity. It finally came to fruition in 1991, when China hosted the first Women's World Cup.

The host country staged an elaborate opening ceremony for the first Women's World Cup.

The tournament put the best female soccer players under the brightest lights. Twelve nations from around the world took part. The games were played at six venues in China's Guangdong region.

Despite having home-field advantage, little was expected of the Chinese squad. China had won the 1991 Asian Championship by defeating Japan, but that result did not guarantee success on the world stage.

Norway was expected to roll through the tournament but the host Chinese team had a surprise in store.

Fewer teams played in the Asian confederation so competition there was not nearly as fierce as it was in other parts of the world.

Most of the pretournament attention was focused on European powerhouses Germany and Norway. The Germans had overcome a 1–0 deficit with three second-half goals to beat Norway 3–1 in the 1991 European Championship. Both teams were expected to have similar success in China.

Norway and China faced off to open the first Women's World Cup on November 16, 1991. But instead of rolling past the host country, Norway stumbled out of the gate. China took a 1–0 lead just 22 minutes in. Then Chinese midfielder Ailing Liu scored twice—once just before halftime and once just after it. Meanwhile, Norway had no answers and couldn't slow down the Chinese team. Qingmei Sun finished the scoring for the hosts, who delivered a 4–0 win over Norway. The upset shocked the world of women's soccer.

But China didn't stop there. The host team moved past the group stage after tying Denmark and defeating New Zealand. Finally, Sweden ended the surprise run by edging China 1–0 in the quarterfinals.

Meanwhile, after losing to China, Norway rebounded with easy wins against New Zealand and Denmark. Norway then defeated Italy in the quarterfinals and Sweden in the semifinals to reach the first ever Women's World Cup final.

Michelle Akers led the United States to victory in the first Women's World Cup final.

Dreams of a rematch of the European final were squelched when the United States drilled Germany 5–2 in the other semifinal. Then the Norwegians lost to the upstart Americans 2–1, giving the United States the first Women's World Cup title.

LI MA STRIKES FIRST

Chinese defender Li Ma cemented her place in Women's World Cup history. She scored the tournament's first goal in China's 4–0 win over Norway. Ma broke through for China in the 22nd minute. Her goal set the stage for one of the biggest upsets in Women's World Cup history.

China came into the tournament relatively unknown in the soccer world, but it went on to show that its performance as the host team was no fluke. The Chinese team finished fourth in the 1995 Women's World Cup. Then they were runners-up to the United States in the 1996 Olympics and the 1999 Women's World Cup.

CHAPTER 4

TRUE NORTH RISES

The 2003 Women's World Cup was thrown into chaos before the tournament could even begin. China was slated to be the host country for the first time since the inaugural Women's World Cup in 1991. However, an outbreak of a deadly virus in China caused a change of venue.

The United States had the infrastructure in place and had shown great support of the tournament when it hosted in 1999. So, the US officials scrambled to put together a

Canada's Christine Latham, *left*, fights for the ball against Germany's Kerstin Stegemann in the 2003 Women's World Cup.

plan to host the 2003 Women's World Cup on short notice. As a result, the tournament was held during the fall in six stadiums across the United States.

This time around, China was one of the favorites, coming off its strong showing in 1999. And the Chinese delivered on those expectations, winning their group with victories over Russia and Ghana and a draw against Australia. It was their fourth straight appearance in the knockout rounds at a Women's World Cup.

Christine Sinclair (12) and Brittany Timko celebrate a goal.

Meanwhile, little was expected of Canada, which had never made it past the group stage. Canada was in a difficult group with powerhouse Germany as well as Japan and Argentina. The Germans were the clear favorites and easily won the group, dispatching Canada 4–1 in the opening match.

But the Canadians were up for the challenge. Forward Christine Latham scored two late goals to seal a 3–0 victory over Argentina, setting up a win-or-go-home match against Japan. The Japanese team jumped ahead with a goal by emerging star Homare Sawa. But Latham scored to pull Canada even before the half. Then Canada's Christine Sinclair, a 20-year-old playing in her first Women's World Cup, scored shortly after the break. Forward Kara Lang added another goal and Canada had a 3–1 victory, clinching its first-ever trip to knockout stage.

China and Canada took the field in the quarterfinals in Portland, Oregon. The Chinese were heavy favorites

REMATCH IN 2015

Canada and China met again in the group stage of the 2015 Women's World Cup. This time it was in Canada, and the home team once again defeated China 1–0. Both squads advanced to the knockout stage that year and lost in the quarterfinals.

because of their past strong performance on the international stage. But the Canadians were undeterred by their long odds. Striker Charmaine Hooper scored in the seventh minute, giving Canada a surprise 1–0 lead. China never recovered from the early deficit and played the rest of the match on its heels. Even with the lead, the Canadians continued to attack. They controlled the pace of play the rest of the match and held on to defeat China 1–0.

The victory sent the Canadians into the semifinals for the first time, but they lost a close match to Sweden, ending their magical run. Through 2015 the fourth-place finish still represented Canada's best Women's World Cup result. Meanwhile, that upset marked the beginning of a slide for the Chinese team. They lost in the quarterfinals in two of the next three Women's World Cups and didn't even qualify for the 2011 tournament.

From left, Andrea Neil, Charmaine Hooper, and Christine Sinclair celebrate Hooper's goal against China.

CHAPTER 5

A HISTORIC TURNAROUND

The Leicester City club has played in the English league system since 1890. But the Foxes aren't one of the league's most successful clubs. In fact, they've spent less than half of that time playing in England's top division, now known as the Premier League. More glamorous clubs such as Manchester United, Chelsea, and Liverpool get most of the attention in the Premier League. But every so often, a team can come out of nowhere to shock the big clubs. Leicester City did just that in 2015–16.

Claudio Ranieri was a calming influence on the Leicester City sidelines.

The Foxes began the campaign as long shots to win a Premier League title. In the previous season, Leicester City was dead last in Premier League standings on Christmas Day. The Foxes faced relegation to a lower division before winning seven of their final nine games to remain in the Premier League. Still, the Foxes were given 5,000-to-1 odds to win the league title before the 2015–16 season began.

Keeper Kasper Schmeichel provided a sturdy backbone to the Leicester City defense.

Leicester named Claudio Ranieri coach before the season. Ranieri had coached many clubs in Europe before taking over the Foxes. Although he was highly respected, Ranieri had never won a top-level championship in Europe. His teams were usually good, but never good enough. Many of Leicester City's fans complained about the Ranieri hire. They claimed the 63-year-old Italian was too old to connect with younger players. They worried his best days were behind him. Much like the Leicester City team itself, Ranieri had much to prove.

The Foxes started the season off with a bang. The team came together nicely as Ranieri settled in. His relaxed approach with the players allowed them to simply focus on the game. Ranieri's tactics also proved successful. His aggressive counterattack philosophy helped confirm the idea that possession of the ball is not always the most important factor in winning. Without a true superstar on the team, the Foxes won 11 of their first 17 games, with five draws and only one loss.

Leicester City's defense rose to the challenge throughout the season. With Danish keeper Kasper Schmeichel in the net and midfielders N'Golo Kanté and Danny Drinkwater helping to control the opposition, the Foxes posted 15 clean sheets, or shutouts, out of 38 league matches. Other talented players emerged seemingly out of nowhere. Strikers Riyad Mahrez and Jamie Vardy provided scoring punch. Vardy scored 24 goals during

SHAKE IT UP

Fans of the Foxes sent literal shockwaves throughout the city during the team's historic run. Students from the University of Leicester installed a seismograph near the Foxes' home at King Power Stadium. Following a goal against Norwich City in February, the seismograph measured a 0.3 quake on the Richter Scale.

Riyad Mahrez kisses the championship trophy after Leicester City's amazing run.

the historic campaign, one shy of the Premier League leader. Mahrez chipped in 17 goals of his own.

By the first week of May, Leicester City had clinched the Premier League championship. All told, the Foxes won 23 games, drew 12, and lost only three in league play, finishing 10 points ahead of second place Arsenal. In the span of just 16 months, Leicester City went from being a candidate for relegation to the best club in England.

CHAPTER 6

THE AMAZING MESSI

Most fans know of Lionel Messi's feats with his Spanish club, FC Barcelona, or the Argentinian national team. Messi is a soccer genius. He is also a global star. His dribbling ability and knack for creating goals are known throughout the world. He set a world record for most goals in a calendar year with 91 in 2012.

Few people, however, realize how much Messi overcame on his way to stardom. In many ways, just being able to play the game was a victory for him.

A 17-year-old Lionel Messi (18) makes a play on the ball for Argentina in a 2005 game against Uruguay.

18
5
5

Messi was born and raised in Argentina. He was diagnosed with growth hormone deficiency as a child. He did not grow as quickly as other kids. Before the age of 10 doctors prescribed a difficult and painful series of injections to deliver medicine he needed to help him grow. “Every night I had to stick a needle into my legs, night after night,” Messi said. He did this for three years. The treatment was painful but effective. He played through the pain and began to gain attention for his skills on the field.

However, the treatment was expensive. It cost approximately $1,500 per month. Government insurance covered part

Messi was an elite scorer from the moment he debuted with Barcelona.

of the costs, but for only two years' worth of treatment. Lionel would need it for several more years. The family struggled to pay. With few options, Lionel's father got help from a hometown soccer club, Newell's Old Boys. The club had been scouting young Lionel. He agreed to play for Newell's, and the club agreed to help pay for the treatment in exchange.

With treatment secure, Lionel focused on growing. And the treatment made him stronger in many ways. He developed a mental

MOVING TO SPAIN

Newell's Old Boys didn't pay for all of Lionel's medical bills. Soon the debt began to pile up for the Messi family. FC Barcelona had gotten word of the great young player from Argentina. The club agreed to pay for the treatment in full if Lionel would join Barcelona. At just 13 years old, he moved to Spain. Lionel finished his final treatment when he was 14 years old and made his pro debut for FC Barcelona shortly after.

Messi's skills on the ball allow him to outmaneuver players much bigger and stronger than he is.

toughness that most kids his age didn't have. Lionel also worked tirelessly at improving his skills. Day after day he practiced the simplest dribbling drills. He soon became so good with the ball at his feet that he could control a game by himself. Other players began to refer to the pesky little player as "the Flea." Lionel realized that his small stature could come in handy.

"I think being smaller than the rest allowed me to be a bit quicker and more agile," he said. Messi learned how to better control the ball because he was closer to the ground. His low center of gravity helped him fight off oncoming defenders.

While playing for Newell's, his dribbling ability turned heads. "Fifteen minutes would go by and he still hadn't lost control of the ball," Gabriel Digeralamo, Messi's old coach at Newell's, said. All of this came from the hard work put in by Messi, thanks in large part to the mental toughness he developed while overcoming a serious health condition.

CHAPTER 7

THE FINAL FRONTIER

Soccer is the most popular game in the world. But it took years for it to catch on in the United States. Professional leagues came and went in the United States, most notably the North American Soccer League (NASL), which began play in 1968. The NASL peaked in the late 1970s when aging international stars such as Pelé, Franz Beckenbauer, and Johan Cruyff arrived to popularize the game in the United States.

Raul Diaz Arce of DC United lifts the MLS Championship Trophy after his side won the league title in 1996.

adidas
21

However, American sports fans didn't fully embrace soccer, preferring to stick with baseball, basketball, football, and hockey. The NASL folded in 1984, and for a time, the only major professional soccer in the United States was the indoor game, played in an arena on a field surrounded by boards.

Professional soccer's comeback began in 1988. When Los Angeles hosted the 1984 Summer Olympics, the soccer matches were an especially big draw. US Soccer officials decided to bid to host the 1994 World Cup. As part of that bid, they agreed to establish a top-tier professional soccer league in the United States. That league would be Major League Soccer (MLS). It began play in 1996 with 10 teams.

Success was not immediate. Attendance was slow to grow. Taking a cue from the NASL, the league tried to import international stars. But none were household names like the players who arrived in the 1970s. Fan support was not there. Unlike in the rest of the world, soccer was not a traditionally popular American sport.

Things began to look up after the 2002 World Cup. The US team fared well in the tournament, making an unexpected run to the quarterfinals. That event helped build momentum for the MLS. More Americans began to watch, both in person and on TV. The 2002 MLS Cup drew the largest attendance for an MLS championship game.

Early support for the league faded quickly—the 1999 MLS All-Star Game was played before a sea of empty seats at San Diego's Qualcomm Stadium.

AMERICANIZING THE GAME

One way MLS tried to appeal to fans was by changing a few rules to make the game seem more familiar to fans of other US sports. One rule introduced a countdown clock instead of a standard clock. Each half started with 45 minutes on the clock and counted down to zero, the opposite of how international soccer is played. Another instituted shootouts to resolve ties. The new rules backfired as the changes alienated traditional fans while not attracting new ones. They were both dropped by the end of the 1999 season.

Slowly but surely the league was growing.

Many markets began to build soccer-specific stadiums. The first team to build its own stadium was the Columbus Crew in 1999. Today many MLS teams have their own venues. A smaller space creates a more raucous atmosphere and makes the games feel like bigger events.

That has helped to grow the league. MLS began play in the 2018 season with 23 teams, including three in Canada. The sport has grown organically. Rivalries have developed. New markets continue to be tapped. Soccer may never be as popular in the United States as the other major professional sports. But there is a place for it, and there's always room for growth.

The response in Seattle and other markets has given soccer fans hope that MLS is here to stay.

GLOSSARY

confederations

The governing bodies of international soccer.

draw

A game that ends in a tie.

equalize

To tie the score in a soccer match.

group stage

The part of a tournament when teams are divided into smaller groups or pools; each team faces the others in its group, and those with the best records move on to the knockout stage.

knockout

A stage of competition when one loss eliminates a team.

midfielder

A player who stays mostly in the middle third of the field and links the defenders with the forwards.

powerhouse

A dominant team.

relegation

Demotion from a higher league to a lower one, usually after finishing at the bottom of the standings.

striker

A forward position in soccer tasked with scoring goals.

MORE INFORMATION

BOOKS

Avise, Jonathan. *Lionel Messi vs. Pelé*. Minneapolis, MN: Abdo Publishing, 2018.

Kortemeier, Todd. *Total Soccer*. Minneapolis, MN: Abdo Publishing, 2017.

Marthaler, Jon. *Ultimate Soccer Road Trip*. Minneapolis, MN: Abdo Publishing, 2019.

ONLINE RESOURCES

Booklinks
NONFICTION NETWORK
FREE! ONLINE NONFICTION RESOURCES

To learn more about soccer underdogs, visit abdobooklinks.com. These links are routinely monitored and updated to provide the most current information available.

INDEX

ABOUT THE AUTHOR

Sam Moussavi is a novelist and freelance writer based in the San Francisco Bay Area. He has written two sets of Young Adult novels as well as many nonfiction sports titles.